300
Incredible Things to Learn on the Internet

300INCREDIBLE.COM, LLC
600 Village Trace, Building 23
Marietta, Georgia 30067

(800) 909-6505

ISBN 1-930435-01-0

— Dedication —

To teachers everywhere, who have worked so hard
to impart the love of learning to us all.

Introduction

Do you have a constant thirst for knowledge? We wrote this book to help you quench it. The Internet is like a vast, uncharted sea, and we want you to use this book as your navigational instrument. Dive in and let the learning begin.

Robyn Spizman
http://www.robynspizman.com

Ken Leebow
Leebow@300INCREDIBLE.COM
http://www.300INCREDIBLE.COM

About the Authors

Robyn Spizman is a consumer advocate with more than seventeen years of experience as "The Super Shopper" and "Super Mom" on network television. Nationally known for her consumer advice, Robyn's lively, high-energy segments have been featured extensively in media appearances on *CNN, The Discovery Channel, CNBC, CNNFN, Roseanne, Good Day New York, ABC Radio Network,* and *National Public Radio.* A former educator, she has authored over sixty books, including award-winning titles in the fields of education, parenting and self help.

Robyn lives in Atlanta with her husband and two children, who get all the credit for helping Mom get online and become a Web wiz.

Ken Leebow has been involved with the computer business for over twenty years. The Internet has fascinated him since he began exploring it several years ago, and he has helped over a million readers utilize its resources. Ken has appeared frequently in the media, educating individuals about the Web's greatest hits. He is considered a leading expert on what is incredible about the Internet.

When not online, you can find Ken playing tennis, running, reading or spending time with his family. He is living proof that being addicted to the Net doesn't mean giving up on the other pleasures of life.

Acknowledgments

Putting a book together requires many expressions of appreciation. The following people deserve our special thanks:

- Robyn's family—Willy, Justin and Ali—for providing steady sources of inspiration and happiness.

- Ken's family—Denice, Alissa and Josh—for being especially supportive during the writing of the book.

- Paul Joffe and Janet Bolton, of *TBI Creative Services*, for their editing and graphics skills.

- Mark Krasner and Janice Caselli for sharing the vision of the book and helping make it a reality.

The Incredible Internet Book Series

300 Incredible Things to Do on the Internet • Volume I

300 More Incredible Things to Do on the Internet • Volume II

300 Incredible Things for Kids on the Internet

300 Incredible Things for Sports Fans on the Internet

300 Incredible Things for Golfers on the Internet

300 Incredible Things for Travelers on the Internet

300 Incredible Things for Health, Fitness & Diet on the Internet

300 Incredible Things for Auto Racing Fans on the Internet

300 Incredible Things for Self-Help & Wellness on the Internet

300 Incredible Things to Learn on the Internet

America Online Web Site Directory
Where to Go for What You Need

1
Acronyms

http://www.acronymfinder.com
Our language contains a lot of alphabet soup. This site lists and defines over 120,000 acronyms.

2
African Americans

http://www.raaheroes.com
http://www.blackvoices.com
http://www.aawc.com
http://www.blackfacts.com
http://www.toptags.com/aama
http://www.pbs.org/wgbh/aia/home.html
http://www.brightmoments.com/blackhistory
http://www.kn.pacbell.com/wired/BHM/AfroAm.html
African American history, culture, accomplishments and contemporary issues can be found here.

3
Alcohol Abuse

http://www.child.net/drugalc.htm
http://www.al-anon-alateen.org
Parents and teens can get the straight facts on drugs and alcohol abuse here, along with useful links and assistance.

4
Algebra

http://www.algebra-online.com
http://www.quickmath.com
Got an Algebra question? This online service can provide the answer.

5
Almanacs

http://kids.infoplease.com
http://www.infoplease.com
These online almanacs have current and historical news on almost every subject.

6
Alphabet

http://www.mrsalphabet.com
If it has to do with the alphabet, you'll find it here. Mrs. Alphabet makes the ABCs informative and fun for kids and adults.

7
Anatomy

http://www.innerbody.com
http://www.medtropolis.com/vbody
Learn about the human body from head to toe.

8
Animals

http://animaldiversity.ummz.umich.edu
The diverse world of animals is explained here.

9
Aquariums

http://matrix.crosswinds.net/~aquarist
http://www.actwin.com/fish
http://www.fishlinkcentral.com
Dive into a sea of details on fresh and saltwater aquarium building and maintenance.

10
Art

http://www.artmuseums.com
http://www.artmuseum.net
http://www.kn.pacbell.com/wired/art2
http://www.artsednet.getty.edu
http://www.crayola.com
Spend some time with these art teachers and museums on the Net.

11
Astronomy

http://tqjunior.advanced.org/3645
http://antwrp.gsfc.nasa.gov/apod/lib/edlinks.html
http://cdsweb.u-strasbg.fr/astroweb.html
http://www.nrao.edu
http://quest.arc.nasa.gov/interactive/hst.html
http://members.aol.com/gca7sky/astrohelp.htm
From daily photographs to explanations of black holes, astronomy is thoroughly examined here.

12
Atlas

http://www.3datlas.com
As the world turns, and names and boundaries change, this atlas site will keep you current with facts and research links for every country. Be sure to check out the area for educators.

13
<u>Attention Deficit Disorder</u>

http://www.oneaddplace.com
http://www.ldonline.org
http://www.adda-sr.org/common.htm
http://www.kidsource.com/feingold/teacher.work.add.html
These are comprehensive sites with articles, resources and support for families dealing with ADHD and other learning difficulties.

14
<u>Authors</u>

http://www.gutenberg.net
http://www.lib.lsu.edu/hum/auth-main.html
http://www.teleport.com/~authilus
From great works of literature to authors who will visit your school, these sites are great reads for everyone.

15
<u>Autism</u>

http://www.autism-resources.com
For those who have children with this condition, or for anyone who wants to learn more about it, you'll find resources ranging from links to books.

16
Automobiles

http://www.innerauto.com
http://www.autoshop-online.com
http://www.alldata.com
Understand how the combustion of gasoline enables us to get from place to place.
Also, learn maintenance and repair and get details about specific vehicles.

17
Aviation

http://www.landings.com
http://www.airliners.net
http://www.planemath.com
http://www.grouper.com/francois
You'll find news, photos and even information about learning to fly. It's almost as
good as being in the cockpit.

18
Babies

http://www.childbirth.org
http://www.pregnancytoday.com
http://www.baby-place.com
How many times have you heard, "They never teach you how to be a parent?" By using the Net, you'll have a great starting point.

19
Ballet

http://www.thepoint.net/~raw/dance.htm
http://www.balletalert.com
http://www.danceart.com
http://www.abt.org/dictionary
These sites are dedicated to dance, complete with history, news, schedules, audition alerts and a dictionary dedicated to keeping dancers and enthusiasts on their toes.

20
Bee's Eye

http://cvs.anu.edu.au/andy/beye/beyehome.html
How does a bee see? The answer is here, and it gives a glimpse into the world of site and perspective.

21
Biography

http://www.biography.com
http://members.home.net/klanxner/lives
http://www.s9.com/biography
http://www.colonialhall.com
Learning about famous people can be fascinating, and these sites have over 20,000 biographies. As a special bonus, check out Colonial Hall and learn all about America's founding fathers.

22
Biology

http://www.hiline.net/~siremba
Mr. Biology offers you practice tests, simplified explanations of hard-to-understand concepts, teacher help and links to exciting Web sites dealing with biology.

23
Birds

http://www.audubon.org
From conservation to the science of birds, it's all here. There are even some special sections for kids and educators.

24
Brain
http://faculty.washington.edu/chudler/neurok.html
Use your brain! This site has been created for students and teachers who want to explore the human nervous system. There are activities and experiments to help learn more about the brain and spinal cord.

25
Butterflies
http://www.butterflyfarm.co.cr
http://www.mesc.usgs.gov/butterfly
http://www.amnh.org/exhibitions/butterflies
How does a caterpillar turn into a butterfly? Do moths have teeth? If you don't know the answers, check out these informative and pretty sites. You can even submit your own questions.

26
Calories
http://www.thriveonline.com/shape/caloriecounter
http://houston.webpoint.com/fitness/calcount.htm
Throughout our life, we hear much about calories. These sites discuss calories and even provide a sample calorie counter for you, based on foods that you enter.

27
Camping

http://www.outdoorexplorer.com
http://www.us-outdoors.com
Before you lace up your boots and hit the trail, check out the gear, weather, available accommodations, restrictions and safety.

28
Camps

http://www.campsearch.com
http://www.kidscamps.com
Pack up your sleeping bag, and head for a summer of fun. Thousands of camps are listed, from residential to day camp to tours and sports camps, conference sites, academic and special needs facilities.

29
Candles

http://www.candles.org
Shine a light on an ancient craft. Learn how to make candles and to use them safely.

30
Candy

http://www.m-ms.com
http://www.jellybelly.com
http://www.candyusa.org
http://www.beakman.com/rock-candy/rock-candy.html
Here's a great way to engage children and adults. Take a virtual tour of some candy favorites. You can even send a candy greeting card. And if you want to make some, Beakman will be happy to assist with rock candy.

31
Capitals

http://www.50states.com
http://www.capitals.com
Here you can match a capital with the state, hear the state song and see many facts and trivia about U.S. states and most countries.

32
Careers

http://jobshadow.monster.com
In the words of Jeff Taylor, CEO of Monster.com, "Career development is a lifelong process that begins years before young adults set out to find their first jobs."

33
Cartoons
http://www.politicalcartoons.com/teacher
This site has developed lesson plans using editorial cartoons as teaching tools in Social Sciences, Art, Journalism and English for all levels.

34
Cells
http://www.cellsalive.com
This fascinating site makes cells come alive for visitors. From magnificent pictures and descriptions to cell cams, you'll enjoy your learning experience here.

35
Cheating
http://www.nocheating.org
This is a campaign to increase awareness about the prevalence of academic cheating and to spark a national discussion of this serious issue.

36
Chemistry

http://www.chem4kids.com
http://www.scimedia.com/chem-ed/scidex.htm
Chemistry is defined here as the study of matter and the changes that take place with that matter. And everything in the universe is made up of matter.

37
Child Statistics

http://www.childstats.gov
This government site offers access to federal and state statistics and reports on children and their families, including: population and family characteristics; economic security; health, behavior and social environment; and education.

38
Children's Health

http://www.kidsdoctor.com
http://www.kidshealth.org
http://www.parentsplace.com/health
These sites are devoted to answering parents' concerns about their kids' health.

"Algebra class will be important to you later in life because there's going to be a test six weeks from now."

39
Civil Rights

http://www.civilrightsphotos.com
If a picture is worth a thousand words, then these pictures of the Civil Rights speak volumes.

40
Civilization

http://www.learner.org/exhibits/collapse
Explore the collapse of four ancient civilizations. You'll learn what happens when a society collapses and how archaeologists find and interpret evidence.

41
Coin Collecting

http://www.coinclub.com
http://www.coin-universe.com
http://www.coinlibrary.com
Coin collecting has always been a favorite hobby. Here are fascinating facts, the latest prices, auction information and an interesting history of the origins of the motto "In God We Trust."

42
College

http://www.petersons.com
http://www.collegeboard.com
http://www.embark.com
http://www.fastweb.com
http://www.finaid.org
http://www.freescholarships.com
There's a lot to learn about colleges. From taking tests to financial aid, it's all here at these sites for the college-bound.

43
College Rankings
http://www.usnews.com/usnews/edu/college/corank.htm
U.S. News and World Report is well-known for its annual college rankings.

44
College Student

http://www.student.com
Students provide this site where other college students can hang out, save money on travel, find out about jobs, pursue internships and participate in work-study programs. Get the latest news on what's going on around town and on campus.

45
Company Profiles

http://profiles.wisi.com/profiles
http://www.companiesonline.com
Find detailed information about thousands of companies.

46
Computer

http://www.computer.com
http://www.computers.com
http://www.cnet.com
http://www.computerlearning.org
Computers can be intimidating and difficult. These sites will assist in learning more about the bits and bytes.

47
Congress
http://www.visi.com/juan/congress
Become an active participant in your government by writing your Congressman. You'll find e-mail addresses and Web sites here.

48
Consumer Education
http://www.pueblo.gsa.gov
http://www.consumerworld.org
http://www.citizen.org
http://www.consumer-action.org
Be the best consumer you can be by reviewing these sites.

49
Conversion
http://www.webcom.com/~legacysy/convert2
http://www.unc.edu/~rowlett/units/index.html
From acceleration to viscosity, you can switch effortlessly between thousands of common and technical English and metric units.

50
Cooking

http://www.goodcooking.com
http://www.globalgourmet.com/destinations
Cooking 101 starts here, with links to the Internet's top food and recipe sites. You'll also find recipes from around the globe.

51
Crafts

http://www.craftcentralstation.com
http://www.craftassoc.com
http://www.craftsfaironline.com
http://craftsforkids.about.com
Get out the glue, sharpen the scissors and get ready to go creative with these thousands of craft ideas.

52
Crime

http://www.mcgruff.org
http://www.ncpc.org
Take a bite out of crime!

53
Critical Thinking…
http://www.criticalthinking.org
…is the art of taking charge of your own mind. If we can take charge of our own minds, we can take charge of our lives, improve them and bring them under our self command and direction.

54
Crystals
http://www.gems4friends.com/therapy.html
http://www.ed.gov/pubs/parents/Science/crystals.html
Learn about the mystical, magical healing properties of crystals and gemstones. You can even learn to grow some in your home or classroom.

55
Currency
http://www.ustreas.gov/education.html
http://www.x-rates.com/calculator.html
Learn about our money and its history. What's the largest denomination currently printed? Also, compare exchange rates from one country to another.

56
Current Events

http://www.publicagenda.org
http://school.newsweek.com
http://www.cagle.com/comics/editorialcontents.asp
What's going on in the world? These sites will keep you informed.

57
DNA

http://vector.cshl.org/dnaftb/asp/splashtable.asp
This site explains DNA, with twenty-four chapters and the use of innovative Internet technology to demonstrate this complex subject. Make sure you view the tutorial before starting your exploration.

58
Dance

http://url.co.nz/arts/dance.html
http://www.sapphireswan.com/dance/styles.htm
Put on your dancing shoes and waltz through these sites. Each of them is filled with highlights, resources and links to every kind of dance imaginable.

59
Debate

http://www.debateinfo.com
Learn about formal debating here.

60
Dental Health

http://www.ada.org/consumer/teachers/index.html
http://www.saveyoursmile.com
http://www.toothfairy.org
Brush up on your dental hygiene.

61
Dictionary

http://www.m-w.com
http://www.onelook.com
http://www.wordcentral.com
http://www.facstaff.bucknell.edu/rbeard/diction.html
These are dream spots for word mavens, scholars and atrocious spellers. The
Merriam-Webster site even allows you to place a dictionary on your browser.

62
Dinosaurs

http://www.dinodon.com
http://dinosaur.umbc.edu
http://dinosaurs.eb.com
http://zoomdinosaurs.com
http://www.dinosaurweb.com
http://palaeo.gly.bris.ac.uk/dinobase/dinopage.html
http://www.nmnh.si.edu/paleo/blast
These sites have detailed illustrations, museum listings, links and even a scientific explanation about the extinction of the dinosaurs.

63
Documents

http://www.thesmokinggun.com
The Smoking Gun is well-known for obtaining and publishing documents that are public record. Some of these documents are interesting in relation to current events and for historical purposes.

64
Dogs

http://www.howtoloveyourdog.com
http://dogs.about.com
http://www.4dogs.com
http://www.dogomania.com
http://www.canismajor.com/dog
These sites will assist all age groups in better understanding our canine friends.

65
Download

http://www.realaudio.com
http://www.adobe.com
http://www.macromedia.com
To make your Internet surfing more enjoyable, download these products. They have become standards on the Net: RealAudio, Acrobat (PDF files) and such Macromedia products as Shockwave and Flash.

66
E-Mail
http://www.iwillfollow.com/emailetiquette.html
http://www.emailhelp.com
http://email.about.com
Here are some sites that offer how-to advice, etiquette and links to sites that will help you personalize your e-mail with graphics, photos and more.

67
Earth
http://www.earth.nasa.gov
To the best of our present knowledge, it is the only place in the universe that can sustain life. Learn more about our planet at this site.

68
Earthquakes
http://www.earthquake.com
http://quake.wr.usgs.gov
http://www.abag.ca.gov/bayarea/eqmaps
Learn about where they often happen, review damage caused by big ones and review what to do if you encounter one.

69
Eclipse

http://www.mreclipse.com
Mr. Eclipse says, "The total eclipse of the Sun is the most spectacular event in all of Nature. Few people have ever witnessed one, but once seen it is an experience never to be forgotten."

70
Economics

http://www.dismal.com
http://www.themint.org
These sites are guaranteed to make economics interesting.

71
Education

http://www.4education.com
http://home.about.com/education
http://www.thinkquest.org
http://www.gsn.org/teach/index.html
These sites will help teachers find some great educational sites on the Net.

72
Education News

http://www.ed.gov
http://www.educationupdate.com
Here you'll find news and information about education.

73
Einstein

http://www.westegg.com/einstein
http://www.pathfinder.com/time/time100/poc/home.html
http://www.rain.org/~karpeles/einsteindis.html
Learn all about the man named "person of the century."

74
Election

http://www.presidentmatch.com
http://selectsmart.com/PRESIDENT
http://www.ivillage.com/election/candidates/match/quiz
These sites ask a few questions to assist you with voting for President of the U.S.

75
Elements

http://www.webelements.com
http://www.cs.ubc.ca/cgi-bin/nph-pertab
http://www.uky.edu/~holler/html/comics.html
Consult the periodic table, with names, symbols, atomic numbers and even cartoons to go with it.

76
Ellis Island

http://www.ellisisland.org
Ellis Island stands as a monument to the immigration history of the United States.

77
Encyclopedias

http://www.britannica.com
http://www.encyclopedia.com
http://www.letsfindout.com
The Internet is itself like a huge encyclopedia, and here are some of the best of the traditional ones.

78
Energy

http://www.energy.ca.gov/education
Learn about energy and famous people who have helped us understand and take advantage if it.

79
England

http://www.bbc.co.uk/education/schools
http://www.schoolzone.co.uk
Get an idea about the education system in England by visiting the award-winning BBC site entitled, "Education—Schools Online." Then, check out one of England's top educational search engines.

80
English as a Second Language

http://www.englishtown.com
http://www.aitech.ac.jp/~iteslj
http://www.gl.umbc.edu/~kpokoy1/grammar1.htm
English is the second language of many students. These sites offer details about grammar, teaching, reading, writing, schools and vocabulary for those students.

"There aren't any icons to click. It's a chalk board."

81
Environment

http://www.envirolink.org
http://www.nceet.snre.umich.edu
http://www.enn.com
http://www.earthsystems.org
Read all about environmental issues and concerns.

82
Ethics

http://ethics.acusd.edu/resources.html
http://www.chem.vt.edu/ethics/ethics.html
Use the Internet to learn about ethics in teaching, research and science.

83
Exploration

http://www.nlc-bnc.ca/dl/1999/passages
From Columbus in 1492, to Amundsen in 1908 and everything in between, it's all here at "A Treasure Trove of North American Exploration."

84
Fairy Tales
http://www.darkgoddess.com/fairy
Fairy tales have enchanted us for a long time, and here are some of the classics.

85
Family Matters
http://www.parentsplace.com
http://www.parentgarden.com
http://www.parentsoup.com
These sites are designed to assist with most issues a family will face.

86
Famous People
http://www.almaz.com/nobel/peace
http://www3.ns.sympatico.ca/educate/people.htm
From Nobel prize winners, to thousands of other famous people, you'll find them here.

87
Fashion

http://www.fashionteen.com
http://www.fashionmall.com
What's happening in the world of fashion? These sites will help keep you tuned in to the trends.

88
Federal Agencies

http://www.fedworld.gov
http://www.fedweb.com/agencylinks.html
http://www.lib.lsu.edu/gov/fedgov.html
The U.S. government has many federal agencies and resources for its citizens. With these sites you're just a link away.

89
Festivals

http://www.festivals.com
http://www.festivalfinder.com
http://www.whatsgoingon.com
Locate thousands of festivals around the world.

90
Film

http://www.learner.org/exhibits/cinema
This site explores the creative process, from the screenwriter's words to the editor's final cut.

91
Fitness

http://www.netsweat.com
http://www.ivillage.com/fitness
These sites can help you lead a healthy lifestyle, covering everything from fitness plans to nutrition.

92
Flags

http://www.usflag.org
http://www.flags.net
http://www.wave.net/upg/immigration/flags.html
http://www.icss.com/usflat/toc.flags.html
http://www.quinnflags.com/flag_etiquette.htm
These sites contain information about flags from all over the world.

93
Food Pyramid

http://www.nal.usda.gov:8001/py/pmap.htm
From breads to fats, the food pyramid has been a guide to proper eating for years.
Now, the power of this pyramid is just a click away.

94
Foreign Language

http://rivendel.com/~ric/resources/dic.html
http://dictionaries.travlang.com
http://translation.langenberg.com
http://www.freetranslation.com
These sites offer dictionaries and translations from one language to another.

95
French

http://www.csbsju.edu/library/internet/french.html
http://www.utm.edu/departments/french/french.html
Ah, the romance of the French language. Start reading, listening and learning today.

96
Galapagos
http://www.pbs.org/saf/5_cool/galapagos/g5_teachers.html
http://www.pbs.org/saf/5_cool/galapagos/g61_links.html
Explore the Galapagos Islands by visiting these sites.

97
Games
http://www.kidsgames.org
Everyone loves a good game, and here are a few that will put a smile on your face.

98
Garbage
http://www.astc.org/exhibitions/rotten/rthome.htm
The old saying, "garbage in, garbage out," doesn't necessarily apply at this site devoted to real trash.

99
Gardening

http://www.vg.com
http://www.gardenweb.com
http://www.gardennet.com
http://www.gardensolutions.com
Here's a great way to relax and discover the wonderful world of gardening.

100
Genealogy

http://www.cyndislist.com
http://cpcug.org/user/jlacombe/mark.html
http://www.myfamily.com
Research your ancestors, and chart your family tree. And with myfamily.com, you can create a Web site that promotes family interaction.

101
Geography

http://www.iln.net/html_p/geography/countries
http://lcweb2.loc.gov/frd/cs/cshome.html
These sites list all countries, from Afghanistan to Zimbabwe.

102
Geometry

http://library.thinkquest.org/20991/geo
http://mathworld.wolfram.com/topics/Geometry.html
This site has been designed for those who may not know all the angles.

103
German

http://web.uvic.ca/german/149
http://www.csbsju.edu/library/internet/german.html
If you're just beginning to learn the German language or need related resources, you'll find it all here.

104
Gifted Children

http://www.nagc.org/ParentInfo
http://www.gifted-children.com
http://www.eskimo.com/~user/kids.html
These sites are exceptional resources for parents, teachers and students.

105
Global Warming

http://www.epa.gov/globalwarming
The EPA says, "The earth's climate is predicted to change, because human activities are altering the chemical composition of the atmosphere through the buildup of greenhouse gases." Learn all about it here.

106
Globe

http://travel.to/globe
This site's goal is to collect examples of the globe for the educational purposes of teaching Earth sciences, geography and cartography.

107
Government

http://www.searchgov.com
http://www.govspot.com
http://world.localgov.org
http://ciir2.cs.umass.edu/Govbot
http://www.thesurfer.com/government
These sites provide resources for local, national and international governments.

108
Graduate School

http://www.petersons.com/graduate
http://www.gre.org
Learn more about graduate schools and the testing process.

109
Grammar

http://www.grammarnow.com
http://www.grammarlady.com
http://www.wsu.edu:8080/~brians/errors/index.html
http://cctc.commnet.edu/HP/pages/darling/grammar.htm
Use these sites to develop a better understanding of, and appreciation for, the English language.

110
Grants

http://www.schoolgrants.org
This site's goal is to contribute to the task of improving schools and programs for the children served by those schools. You'll find resources for children, educators and K-12 schools.

111
Greece

http://www.perseus.tufts.edu
The Perseus Project is a resource for the study of the ancient world. You will find a huge collection of information on the Archaic and Classical Greek world.

112
Handwriting

http://www.parkerpen.co.uk/history
The well-known pen company provides a brief and interesting history and timeline of over 25,000 years of writing.

113
Health

http://www.kidshealth.org
http://www.healthgate.com
http://www.4healthandfitness.com
http://www.netwellness.com
http://www.webMD.com
The Internet has many useful resources to help us all be well.

114
Health Care for Pets
http://www.petdental.com
http://www.netpaws.com
Give your pets the care they deserve.

115
Heart
http://sln.fi.edu/biosci/heart.html
In an average lifetime, the human heart beats more than two and a half billion times, without pausing to rest. Learn all about your heart here.

116
Herbs
http://onhealth.com/ch1/resource/herbs
http://botanical.com/botanical/mgmh/mgmh.html
Before you start chewing the shrubbery, find out about the uses of herbs and other natural materials.

117
Highway Safety

http://www.dot.gov
http://www.nhtsa.dog.gov
http://www.hwysafety.org
http://www.aaafts.org
Everything you need to know about highway and automobile safety is addressed at these sites.

118
Hispanic

http://www.neta.com/~1stbooks/index.html
http://www.hisp.com
http://www.hispanic.com/content_main.htm
This site showcases Hispanic culture, history, news, politics and organizations—in both English and Español.

"IF YOU MISS ME WHEN I GO AWAY TO COLLEGE, JUST VISIT MY WEB PAGE AND CLICK THE AUDIO FILE TO HEAR ME YELL AT YOU."

119
History

http://www.yale.edu/lawweb/avalon/avalon.htm
http://www.thehistorynet.com
http://www.historyplace.com
http://www.hyperhistory.com
http://www.talkinghistory.org
http://www.mnh.si.edu/museum/online.html
http://www.geocities.com/Athens/Academy/6617/whgen.html
"We can chart our future clearly and wisely only when we know the path which has led to the present." —Adlai E. Stevenson

120
History in Film

http://www.historyinfilm.com
This site focuses on the historical content, educational value and lessons that can be learned from some famous movies.

121
Holocaust

http://www.holocaustsurvivors.org
Read the stories of the survivors, hear them speak, look at their family photographs and read a historical introduction to the Holocaust. And when you're done, leave your thoughts or ask your questions.

122
Homework

http://www.kidsvista.com
http://www.studyweb.com
http://www.homeworkheaven.com
http://www.refdesk.com/homework.html
These sites are great resources for help with homework.

123
Human Rights

http://www.oneworld.net
This organization's goal is to "bear witness to the injustices and unnecessary suffering in the world."

124
Humanities

http://www.neh.gov
http://edsitement.neh.gov/websites-lit.htm
The National Endowment for the Humanities brings you the best of the humanities on the Web. It is a collection of valuable online resources for teaching English, history, art history and foreign languages.

125
Illusions

http://www.illusionworks.com
http://www.sandlotscience.com
http://www.lainet.com/illusions/links.htm
What you see is not always what you get. These sites examine and explain optical effects and illusions in science and nature.

126
Innovation

http://www.thetech.org/exhibits_events/online/tech10
Each month, the Tech Museum of Innovation presents ten excellent Web sites that focus on high technology and innovation.

127
Insects

http://www.insects.org
Spend a few moments here, and learn how to appreciate the significance of these miniature marvels.

128
Internet 101

http://www.webteacher.org
http://www.school.com
http://l2lpd.arin.k12.pa.us/linktuts/bgtoc.htm
http://www2.famvid.com/i101/internet101.html
http://www.netlingo.com
Are you new to the Internet, or do you know someone who is? Use these sites to get up to speed.

129
Internet Safety

http://www.safekids.com
http://www.virtuocity.com/family
Consult these sites that effectively promote safe Web surfing and how to be a responsible Netizen.

130
Inventors and Inventions

http://www.inventorsdigest.com
http://www.invent.org
http://www.inventamerica.com
http://web.mit.edu/invent
Your creativity will be energized by these amazing inventors and inventions.

131
Journalism

http://www.journalismnet.com
Gain insight into news and issues from a wide variety of sources.

132
Karate

http://www.usakarate.org
http://maxpages.com/superkicker/Karate_Links
Karate provides us with the opportunity to learn about discipline, self-confidence and health.

133
Keyboarding
http://www.absurd.org/jb/typodrome
Try this site to test your typing skills.

134
Language
http://www.m-w.com
http://www.thesaurus.com
http://www.itools.com/research-it
These reference sites are at your disposal to help find a word, pronounce it, define it, rhyme it or rephrase it.

135
Latin
http://www.csbsju.edu/library/internet/latin.html
http://www.nd.edu/~archives/latgramm.htm
http://humanum.arts.cuhk.edu.hk/Lexis/Latin
The Latin language is alive and well on the Internet.

136
Law

http://www.findlaw.com
http://www.laweasy.com/ii.htm
http://www.nolo.com
http://www.ncjrs.org
How many lawyers does it take to find the best legal sites? None; we've already done it for you here.

137
Learning

http://www.4learning.com
http://www.learn2.com
http://www.games2learn.com
These resource sites will assist your quest for knowledge.

138
Legends and Myths
http://www.stemnet.nf.ca/CITE/legends.htm
http://www.legends.dm.net
Visit the world of magic and myth with stories from around the globe.

139
Lesson Plans

http://www.homeworkcentral.com/teachers
http://school.discovery.com
http://www.pbs.org/teachersource
http://www.nytimes.com/learning/teachers/lessons
http://ericir.syr.edu/Virtual/Lessons
http://encarta.msn.com/schoolhouse
http://educate.si.edu/resources/lessons/lessons.html
http://www.nationalgeographic.com/resources/ngo/education/ideas.html
Thousands of lesson plans for every subject can be found at these sites designed for the educator.

140
Librarians

http://www.lii.org
http://www.libraryspot.com
http://www.servtech.com/public/mvail/home.html
The Internet is the largest library in the world, but no one is actually in charge of organizing it. These folks are doing their best.

141
Library

http://www.4libraries.com
http://lcweb.loc.gov
http://sunsite.berkeley.edu/Libweb
These sites will take you to libraries from the "bricks and mortar" world that have an online presence.

142
Literacy

http://literacynet.org/cnnsf
Courtesy of CNN, you can read stories in categories ranging from adventure to science, then test yourself for comprehension.

143
Literature

http://www.bartleby.com/cambridge
Enjoy the Cambridge history of English and American literature.

144
Literature, American
http://www.usia.gov/products/pubs/oal/oaltoc.htm
http://www.usia.gov/products/pubs/oal/amlitweb.htm
http://www.csustan.edu/english/reuben/pal/TABLE.HTML
Here's a history of American Literature, featuring many of the great writers who have been a part of it.

145
Literature, British
http://andromeda.rutgers.edu/~jlynch/Lit/20th.html
Jack Lynch, an English professor, maintains many excellent Web sites on the Net. This one concentrates on resources for English Lit.

146
Literature, Children's
http://www.carolhurst.com
http://www.acs.ucalgary.ca/~dkbrown
http://planetpostcard.com/childlit/childlit.html
Get reviews and resources for children's literature, and sift through ideas of how to use these books in the classroom.

147
Magazines

http://www.magazine-rack.com
http://www.zinezone.com
There are thousands of magazines online, and at the ZineZone, you can even create your own.

148
Maps

http://www.mapquest.com
http://www.mapblast.com
http://maps.expedia.com
http://terraserver.microsoft.com
http://www.nationalgeographic.com/resources/ngo/maps
http://www.usgs.gov/education/learnweb/Maps.html
These maps should complement any school report or project.

149
Mars

http://www.mars2030.net
Will we colonize Mars by the year 2030? This creative and educational site explores the possibilities.

150
Math

http://www.cut-the-knot.com
http://mathworld.wolfram.com
http://www-sci.lib.uci.edu/SEP/math.html
http://forum.swarthmore.edu
http://www.webmath.com
http://www.sisweb.com/math/tables.htm
http://tqjunior.advanced.org/4116
These sites feature all types of mathematics for every educational level.

151
Math Fun

http://www.mathgoodies.com
http://personal.cfw.com/~clayford
http://tqjunior.thinkquest.org/4116
http://www.learner.org/exhibits/dailymath
Enjoy the practical and enjoyable applications of math.

152
Mazes
http://www.flint.umich.edu/Departments/ITS/crac/maze.form.html
Once you enter into this fascinating world of mazes, you may never want to find your way out.

153
Media
http://www.mediachannel.org
It's important to keep an active watch on the media, and all eyes are open at the Media Channel.

154
Medicine
http://www.nlm.nih.gov
http://www.drkoop.com
http://www.mdadvice.com
Get a dose of advice, drug information, journals, doctors and health news here.

155
Memory
http://www.exploratorium.edu/memory
Don't forget to learn all about human memory here.

156
Mental Health
http://www.mentalhelp.net
http://www.mhsource.com
http://www.psychcentral.com/web.htm
These sites offer many resources about mental health issues.

157
Microbes
http://commtechlab.msu.edu/sites/dlc-me/zoo
Visit the microbe zoo, and learn about the microorganisms that are important to us.

158
Military

http://www.military-network.com
http://www.militarycareers.com
These sites offer a glimpse into the armed forces, including careers in the military.

159
Milk

http://www.moomilk.com
Get a fun and interesting virtual tour, and learn all about cows and milk.

160
Monticello

http://www.monticello.org
Visit the home of Thomas Jefferson and learn about his life. Monticello is the only house in America on the United Nations' prestigious World Heritage List of places that must be protected at all costs.

"THIS IS THE FINEST, MOST COMPREHENSIVE AND INFORMATIVE TERM PAPER I'VE EVER READ. BUT YOU WERE SUPPOSED TO WRITE ABOUT 'PLATO' NOT 'PLAYDOUGH'."

161
Multiculturalism
http://curry.edschool.virginia.edu/go/multicultural/teachers.html
Barbara Jordan said, "America's mission was and still is to take diversity and mold it into a cohesive and coherent whole." Teachers can use this site to achieve this goal in their classrooms.

162
Museums
http://www.museumlink.com
http://wwar.com/museums.html
http://www.amnh.org
http://www.metmuseum.org
These are a few examples of magnificent museums that can also be accessed online.

163
Music
http://www.music-ed-directory.com
http://www.siba.fi/Kulttuuripalvelut/music.html
http://www.music.com
These sites provide enough links to satisfy fans of any type of music.

164
Myths
http://www.pantheon.org/mythica/areas
From Aboriginal to Roman, explore ancient mythology here.

165
Names
http://www.behindthename.com
http://clanhuston.com/name/name.htm
Discover the history and meaning of people's names.

166
Native Americans
http://www.dickshovel.com/www.html
http://www.turtle-tracks-for-kids.org
Become more familiar with Native Americans, from the Abenaki to the Winnebago.

167
Nature

http://www.panda.org
http://www.naturepark.com
http://www.greatoutdoors.com
http://www.fs.fed.us/outdoors/naturewatch
Become more familiar with what's happening to our planet, its seas, the forests and the global climate.

168
News

http://www.newseum.org
http://www.cnn.com
http://abcnews.go.com
http://cbsnews.cbs.com
http://nt.excite.com
http://www.msnbc.com/news/learning_front.asp
Receive all your news online.

169
News, Satirical

http://www.theonion.com
http://www.wackytimes.com
Many of these satirical issues and articles can be used for discussion and other educational purposes.

170
Newsletters

http://www.surfnetkids.com
http://scout.cs.wisc.edu/caservices/net-hap/index.html
These newsletters will keep you informed about great educational sites on the Net. Go ahead and subscribe; they're free.

171
Newspapers

http://www.thepaperboy.com
http://www.totalnews.com
http://www.newsdirectory.com
If a newspaper is available on the Net, you'll find it here. These are great sites to use for research projects.

172
Numbers
http://www.zompist.com/numbers.shtml
http://www.ontko.com/~rayo/primes/index.html
Learn to count to ten in over 4,000 languages, and learn all about prime numbers.

173
Nutrition
http://www.kidsfood.org
http://www.nutritionnewsfocus.com
http://navigator.tufts.edu
http://www.nutri-facts.com
http://library.thinkquest.org/10991
Good nutrition is important to living a healthy lifestyle. These sites provide detailed information and even a few lesson plans.

174
Oceans
http://www.ocean.udel.edu/deepsea
http://oceanlink.island.net
http://seawifs.gsfc.nasa.gov/ocean_planet.html
Dive into a sea of knowledge about our oceans.

175
Occupations
http://cbweb9p.collegeboard.org/career/bin/career.pl
Get a head start by looking at career choices now.

176
Oddities
http://www.ghosts.org
http://www.improb.com
http://www.paradigmshift.com
http://www.unmuseum.org
http://www.activemind.com/Mysterious
Albert Einstein said, "The most beautiful thing we can experience is the mysterious. It is the source of all true art and science."

177
Olympic Games
http://www.olympic.org
http://www.olympic-usa.org
http://devlab.cs.dartmouth.edu/olympic
Take a marathon look at the myths, facts, history and statistics of the ancient and modern Olympic Games.

178
Origami

http://www.origami-usa.org
http://www.origami.vancouver.bc.ca
http://www.the-village.com/origami
Who would think that a simple sheet of paper could become a shark, flower, crane, box or whatever—all without scissors or tape? Visit these sites to learn the ancient Japanese art of paper folding.

179
Outdoors

http://www.alloutdoors.com
http://www.gorp.com
http://www.outdoors.net
If you can't be outdoors, you can at least spend some time at these sites that are about the outdoors.

180
Paper

http://www.grice.net/paper.htm
Learn everything you ever needed to know about paper at this site.

181
Parenting

http://www.fcs.wa.gov.au/parenting/tips/default.htm
http://www.parents-talk.com
http://www.parentingteens.com
http://www.tnpc.com
These sites will inform, entertain and make you think carefully about the tremendous responsibility of parenting.

182
Patents

http://www.patentcafe.com
http://www.patents.ibm.com
Check out the world of patents, inventors and inventions, including a "Gallery of Obscure Patents" and "The Wacky Patent of the Month."

183
Pen Pals

http://www.epals.com
http://www.andys-penpals.com
http://amifriend.virtualave.net/penpal/eindex.htm
Are you curious about people around the world? These sites will help you find a pen pal from another country.

184
Pencil

http://www.pencils.com
You use it all day long. Now, learn from Dr. Petroski everything you ever needed to know about this incredible writing device.

185
Pets

http://www.apapets.com
http://www.petsource.com
http://www.acmepet.com
At these excellent sites, learn how to keep your pets healthy and happy.

186
Pharmacist

http://www.rxlist.com
http://www.pharminfo.com/drg_mnu.html
Get specific information about prescription drugs. You'll find helpful details about usage, side effects and more.

187
Philosophy

http://www.trincoll.edu/depts/phil/philo/index.html
http://www.geocities.com/Athens/Delphi/2795/home.htm
I think, therefore I am—able to find just about anything about philosophy and philosophers at these sites.

188
Photography

http://www.shortcourses.com
http://www.mediahistory.com/photo.html
Learn all about photography, including the newest digital cameras.

189
Physics

http://www.physlink.com
http://www.kent.wednet.edu/staff/trobinso/physicspages/PhysicsOf.html
http://www.learner.org/exhibits/parkphysics
Physics can be fun. These sites will prove that theory to you.

190
Pimple Portal

http://www.pimpleportal.com
http://kidshealth.org/kid/normal/acne.html
Here are causes, treatments and resources for the 17,000,000 people with acne.

191
Planets

http://seds.lpl.arizona.edu/nineplanets/nineplanets
http://www.iln.net/main/astronomy/planets.asp
Get an overview of the history, mythology and current scientific knowledge about
the planets and moons in our solar system.

192
Plants

http://plants.usda.gov
http://garden-gate.prairienet.org
http://tqjunior.thinkquest.org/3608
Here are some great spots to dig for information about plants and plant care.

193
Poetry

http://www.pw.org
http://www.poetrysociety.org
http://www.poems.com
http://www.favoritepoem.org
http://www.hti.umich.edu/english/amverse
http://www.geocities.com/~spanoudi/poems/index.html
These sites will expose you to the joys of poetry and many of the well-known poets.

194

Poison

http://www.ipl.org/youth/poisonsafe/pother.html
http://www.enviroderm.com/poison.htm
http://www.botanical.com/botanical/mgmh/poison.html
Find information on avoiding poisonous plants and what to do if you accidentally swallow, touch or breathe poisonous substances.

195

Political Science

http://pslab11.polsci.wvu.edu/PolyCy
http://users.erols.com/irasterb/gov.htm
http://thomas.loc.gov
You'll vote "yes" for these sites that detail the workings of government and the principles of political science.

"My mom got me this game. Every time you blow up an alien, you have to stop and clean up the mess before you can continue to play."

196
Politics

http://www.aboutpolitics.com
http://www.allpolitics.com
http://www.stm.it/politic
http://www.trytel.com/~aberdeen
While some people may be apathetic about politics, these sites express a passion for the subject.

197
Population

http://www.popnet.org
The world population is six billion and growing. You'll find information, demographics and many other population-related Web sites here.

198
Portals

http://www.kidsvista.com
Designed for educators and kids, this site and other portals will help provide a comprehensive learning experience on the Net.

199
Presidents

http://www.npg.si.edu/col/pres
http://gi.grolier.com/presidents/preshome.html
http://metalab.unc.edu/lia/president
http://www.synnergy.com/day/prestc.htm
http://www.pathfinder.com/offers/presidents
Get to know more about the U.S. presidents, from their official portraits to detailed biographical information.

200
Projects

http://www.schoolworld.asn.au
Become involved with a worthwhile project by using the Internet as a resource.

201
Psychology

http://www.thepsych.com
http://www.psych-central.com
http://www.psychwww.com
Sign up for Psych 101 at these sites.

202
Publications

http://www.publist.com
Search a database of over 150,000 magazines, journals, newsletters and other periodicals. Find in-depth information from familiar and hard-to-find publications around the world, representing thousands of topics.

203
Puppetry

http://www.sagecraft.com/puppetry
http://home.carolina.rr.com/puppetrylounge
http://www3.ns.sympatico.ca/onstage/puppets
No strings attached, these are some terrific resources for anyone interested in this ancient art.

204
Questions

http://www.askjeeves.com
AskJeeves.com is the best site on the Net that actually answers your questions by guiding you to specific sites.

205
Quiz
http://www.quizsite.com
http://www.naturalland.com/quizzes.htm
http://www.mtwilson.edu/Education/ConQuiz
http://abc.go.com/primetime/millionaire
Quizzes can be fun and educational. If you're good enough, you might even get to appear on the "Who Wants to be a Millionaire?" TV show.

206
Quotations
http://www.searchgateway.com/phrases.htm
http://www.quoteland.com
http://www.aphids.com/quotes/index.shtml
http://www.startingpage.com/html/quotations.html
If you can't find a way to express it at these sites, it may not be worth saying.

207
Radio

http://www.virtualtuner.com
http://www.netradio.net
http://wmbr.mit.edu/stations/list.html
Listen to the radio—on your computer, and learn the history of the first broadcast medium of mass communication.

208
Rainbows

http://www.zianet.com/rainbow/boInfo.htm
http://www.unidata.ucar.edu/staff/blynds/rnbw.html
A rainbow is "one of the most spectacular light shows observed on earth." Learn all about them here.

209
Reading

http://www.toread.com
http://www.rhlschool.com/reading.htm
http://www.readbygrade3.com
These lessons, aids and reading lists will help encourage youngsters to delve into the wonderful world of books.

210
Recycling

http://www.recycle.net
http://www.libsci.sc.edu/bob/RECYCLE.HTM
http://www.epa.gov/recyclecity
http://users.hsonline.net/kidatart
Become an active part of the recycling movement. You'll even find out how to make art out of garbage.

211
Reference

http://www.refdesk.com
http://www.ipl.org/ref
The Internet is a massive reference resource, and these sites will click you in the right directions.

212
Renaissance

http://www.learner.org/exhibits/renaissance
The Renaissance was the age in which artistic, social, scientific, and political thought turned to major new directions. Learn all about Europe's rebirth.

213
Research

http://www.researchpaper.com
Visit the Research Paper, and find a collection of topics, ideas and assistance for school-related projects.

214
Resources, Parents

http://www.tnpc.com
http://www.ala.org/parents
http://www.kidsource.com/subscribe.html
Parents will find newsletters, Web sites and other interesting articles to assist in the vital process of education.

215
Resources, Students

http://www.netguide.com/kids
http://www.pinkmonkey.com
http://www.bjpinchbeck.com
http://www.iln.net/main/research
These sites will help students hone in on resource sites that are worth visiting.

216
Resources, Teachers

http://www.ed.gov/free/subject.html
http://www.ozline.com/learning/theory.html
http://learn.msn.com/teachers/directory.asp

Teachers can use these resources to understand the Internet and how to utilize it as a research tool.

217
Rhymes

http://www.writeexpress.com/online.html

This site will help you find rhyming words.

218
Robots

http://ranier.hq.nasa.gov/telerobotics_page/coolrobots.html

See which Web sites have achieved "Cool Robot of the Week" honors for featuring and promoting robotics systems, solutions, technology and information.

219
Royalty

http://www.royalarchive.com
http://www.geocities.com/Athens/Aegean/7545
Kings and queens and other royalty of all eras and countries are featured here.

220
SAT

http://www.powerprep.com/tipofday.shtml
http://www.testprep.com/wwmain.sat.html
Get preparation tips, and take sample SAT tests.

221
Safety

http://www.cpsc.gov
http://www.fema.gov/kids
http://www.fsis.usda.gov
http://www.nhtsa.dot.gov/kids
http://msf-usa.org/pages/MAIN1.html
http://www.nssl.noaa.gov/~nws/safety.html
http://www.ou.edu/oupd/kidsafe/start.htm

These sites are devoted to keeping you out of harm's way at home, at work, on the roads, in the water, in the kitchen and wherever else you go and whatever else you do.

222
Satellite

http://www.thetech.org/hyper/satellite

Technically, satellites are any objects that orbit or revolve around other objects. This site provides details about the kind that orbit our planet.

223
Science

http://www.sciencedaily.com
http://www.sciencegems.com
http://www.wsu.edu/DrUniverse
You'll find answers to science questions and up-to-the-minute research news.

224
Science Fair Projects

http://www.stemnet.nf.ca/~jbarron/scifair.html
http://sciencefairproject.virtualave.net
Stuck for an original idea? Check here for topics, outlines and hints for producing a successful science fair project.

225
Scientist

http://www.madsci.org
This site uses the Internet to unite hundreds of scientists in a forum where people can ask questions and learn more about the world around them. The accumulated body of information is maintained as a resource for all.

226
Scouting

http://www.bsa.scouting.org
http://www.girlscouts.org
Scouting has been a major force for kids since the early 1900s. From cookies to volunteering, it's all here for boys, girls and adults, too.

227
Scrapbooks

http://www.learn2scrapbook.com
http://www.scrapbookideas.com
http://www.scrapbooking.com
Find tons of ideas here to help organize and preserve your precious memories and favorite collections.

228
Search Engines
http://www.searchengineshowdown.com
http://www.altavista.com
http://www.excite.com
http://www.lycos.com
http://www.search.com
http://www.yahoo.com
Can't find something on the Net? With links to over one billion Web pages, these search engines should be able to provide some assistance.

229
Search Engine, Education Sites
http://www.searchedu.com
There are over 20 million university and education pages indexed and ranked in order of popularity.

230
Search Engine, Lesson Plans
http://www.virtuallrc.com/lessonplans.html
There are many sites on the Net that offer lesson plans. This one offers the ability to search them.

231
Search Engines, Meta

htto://www.dogpile.com
http://www.northernlight.com
http://www.profusion.com
http://www.metacrawler.com
http://www.ajkids.com
These will search multiple search engines simultaneously.

232
Self-Esteem

http://www.self-worth.com
http://www.learner.org/exhibits/personality
The dictionary defines self-esteem as "confidence and satisfaction in oneself."
Boost yours here.

233
Seminar Finders

http://www.seminarfinder.com
http://www.onlearning.net
Use these sites to find seminars you may want to attend.

234
Senior Citizens

http://www.eldernet.com
http://www.senior.com
http://www.seniors.com
Seniors can use these guides to health, housing, financial, lifestyle and retirement news, with free newsletters and health advice.

235
Senses

http://www.hhmi.org/senses
Anything we see, hear, feel, smell, or taste requires billions of nerve cells to flash urgent messages along cross-linked pathways and feedback loops in our brains, performing intricate calculations that scientists have only begun to decipher. Wow!

"To upgrade or not to upgrade, that is the question!"

236
Shakespeare

http://www.theplays.org
http://tech-two.mit.edu/Shakespeare/works.html
http://www.bartleby.com/99/138.html
http://daphne.palomar.edu/shakespeare
Here are the complete works of William Shakespeare and a comprehensive guide to Shakespeare sites on the Net, with a timeline, genealogy and even a biography quiz.

237
Shareware

http://tukids.tucows.com
http://www.shareware.com
http://www.download.com
Downloading software via the Net has become very easy and popular.

238
Shopping

http://www.schoolpop.com
Make a purchase at Schoolpop.com, and it will make a contribution to your school.

239
Short Stories
http://www.bnl.com/shorts
If you have only a little free time, read some classic short stories. You'll also find brief biographies and links to other worthwhile sites.

240
Sign Language
http://www.handilinks.com/hand/sign.htm
http://www.bconnex.net/~randys
http://commtechlab.msu.edu/sites/aslweb
Learn to say it with your hands.

241
Social Studies
http://www.execpc.com/~dboals/boals.html
Join Mr. Boals as he encourages you to use the Internet as a tool for learning and teaching history and social studies.

242
Solar System

http://www.solarviews.com
http://space.jpl.nasa.gov
http://maps.jpl.nasa.gov

Discover the latest scientific information, or study the history of space exploration, rocketry, early astronauts, space missions, and spacecraft through a vast archive of photographs, scientific facts, text, graphics and videos.

243
Sonnets

http://www.sonnets.org

Sonnet Central is an archive of English sonnets, commentary, pictures and relevant Web links.

244
Space

http://www.nasa.gov
http://www.thespaceplace.com
http://www.space.com
http://www.nasm.edu
http://www.seds.org
Enjoy these sites that bring outer space closer to home.

245
Spanish

http://www.kn.pacbell.com/wired/fil/pages/listspanish.html
http://www.studyspanish.com
These sites are good resources for students who speak Spanish as their primary
language, and for those learning Spanish as a foreign language.

246
Speeches

http://douglass.speech.nwu.edu
From the 1600s to the present, you can read these famous speeches.

247
Spelling

http://www.spellingbee.com
http://webster.commnet.edu/hp/pages/darling/grammar/spelling.htm
Join a spelling bee or just take some lessons or quizzes.

248
Sports

http://espn.go.com
http://www.sportsline.com
http://www.foxsports.com
http://ww.cnnsi.com
Take a little time to keep current about major sporting events.

249
Stamp Collecting

http://www.ioa.com/~ggayland/junior
http://www.philately.com
http://collectstamps.about.com
Whether you're just a beginning philatelist or an old pro, these sites will help with
your hobby.

250
Statistics
http://www.lib.umich.edu/libhome/Documents.center/stats.html
Here's statistical information about subjects from "agriculture" to "weather."

251
Statue of Liberty
http://www.libertystatepark.com
http://www.nyctourist.com/liberty1.htm
Next to the flag, this inspiring icon for immigrants is America's most famous symbol of freedom.

252
Stock Market
http://library.thinkquest.org/10326
http://www.smg2000.org
http://www.fantasystockmarket.com
You're never too young to learn about the stock market. These sites will assist teachers and students in learning how it all works.

253
Study Guides

http://www.iss.stthomas.edu/studyguides
http://www.eop.mu.edu/study
http://www.thespark.com/sparknotes
These sites offer strategies to make your learning efforts more effective.

254
Teachers

http://www.pitsco.com/p/resframe.htm
http://www.teacher.com/act.htm
http://www.learningspace.org
http://www.teachers.net
http://www.eduhound.com
http://www.ceismc.gatech.edu/busyt
http://www.teachervision.com
http://www.education-world.com
All of these sites are intended to make an educator's life a little easier.

255
Technology

http://www.eschoolnews.org
This site discusses many of the current issues in technology.

256
Teens

http://www.wa.gov/ago/youth
http://www.ipl.org/teen
http://www.teens.com
http://www.bolt.com
http://www.channelone.com
No lectures here, just good common sense and interesting topics for teens.

257
Telephone

http://www.cavejunction.com/phones
Visit the Cyber Telephone Museum to learn about the origins and evolution of this vital communication device.

258
Test – Assessment

http://www.escore.com
A child can take a free assessment test here to get an educational snapshot of where he stands.

259
Tests – Personality

http://www.2h.com/Tests/iq.phtml
http://www.davideck.com
Test for your IQ, personality, career and many other interesting and fun things.

260
Think!

http://www.encyclozine.com/Puzzle
This site states, "A puzzle is a mental challenge, usually suitable for one person to solve alone." Enjoy perplexing puzzles that will get all ages thinking.

261
Time

http://www.isbister.com/worldtime
http://tycho.usno.navy.mil/time.html
Does anybody really know what time it is? These folks do.

262
Toys

http://www.drtoy.com
http://www.toysfortots.org
Dr. Toy discusses the best toys and where to get them, while the Marines tell you how to donate toys to underprivileged kids through Toys for Tots.

263
Travel

http://travel.roughguides.com
http://expedia.msn.com
http://www.previewtravel.com
http://www.frommers.com
http://www.fodors.com
http://www.travelocity.com
http://www.thetrip.com
These are excellent sites that will help with your travel plans.

264
Trivia

http://www.funtrivia.com
http://www.absolutetrivia.com
http://www.triviaworld.com
http://www.scholarstuff.com/netguide/trivia/trivia.htm
In pursuit of the trivial, have fun and learn a lot of miscellaneous facts.

265
Tutor

http://www.iln.net
Meet the Internet tutor.

266
UFO

http://www.cninews.com
http://www.xproject-paranormal.com
Do you believe in Unidentified Flying Objects? These sites do.

267
Ultrasound

http://www.cs.uwa.edu.au/~bernard/us3d.html
http://www.ob-ultrasound.net
Get all the information you want about ultrasound, from its history to its uses in medicine today.

268
Unions

http://www.unions.org
http://www.aflcio.org
Learn about labor unions and their purposes.

269
United Nations

http://www.un.org
http://www.unsystem.org
http://www.unol.org
The UN is central to global efforts to solve problems that challenge humanity. It works to promote respect for human rights, protect the environment, fight disease, promote development and reduce poverty.

"There's no such thing as a free education. You have to pay attention."

270
United States of America

http://www.usia.gov
http://www.nara.gov
http://www.geocities.com/Athens/Forum/9061/USA/usa.html
http://www.census.gov
View the country from many different angles — geographical, cultural, natural, historic, environmental and, of course, its people.

271
Urban Studies

http://www.urban.org
http://npc.press.org/library/healy.htm
http://www.bestpractices.org
Get acquainted with current trends in urban studies, crime and social services.

272
Vaccines

http://www.immunofacts.com
http://www.cdc.gov/nip/vacsafe/fs/vaxsaft.htm
http://www.vaccines.com
Get detailed doses of information and news about the world of vaccines.

273
Values

http://www.uia.org/values/webval.htm
http://www.usia.gov/usa/socval.htm
Examine issues ranging from family values to global concerns.

274
Vegetarianism

http://www.veg.org/veg
http://www.vegweb.com
http://www.vrg.org
These sites are devoted to the vegetarian lifestyle. You'll find recipes and answers to many of your questions.

275
Veterinarians

http://www.avma.org/defaultmain.html
Animal lovers will enjoy this site dedicated to the doctors who help pets.

276
Violence

http://www.child.net/violence.htm
These resources can help you learn what fosters violence, what can be done to prevent it and how to begin conflict resolution to keep our kids safe.

277
Vitamins

http://www.vitaminbuzz.com
http://www.realtime.net/anr/vitamins.html
http://www.realtime.net/anr/minerals.html
Take a dose of this supplementary reading about vitamins, minerals and herbs that may help keep you healthy.

278
Vocabulary

http://www.vokabel.com
http://www.vocabulary.com
http://www.randomhouse.com/wotd
http://www.fun-with-words.com
Build your vocabulary with word exercises, puzzles and games.

279
Volcano

http://volcano.und.nodak.edu
http://www.geo.mtu.edu/volcanoes
These sites contain detailed information about volcanoes around the world.

280
Voting

http://www.fec.gov
http://www.womenvote.org
http://www.vote-smart.org
Learn all about voting procedures from the Federal Election Commission, and become a more-informed voter by following candidates and the election process.

281
Walking

http://www.walkingconnection.com
http://www.teleport.com/~walking/hiking.html
http://walking.about.com
http://www.racewalk.com
Let the Net teach you all about walking for health and exercise.

282
War

http://www.wtj.com/portal

Here's a resource for researchers, hobbyists, armed forces professionals and all others with an interest in military history, science and defense.

283
Washington, D.C.

http://sc94.ameslab.gov/TOUR/tour.html
http://xroads.virginia.edu/~CAP/title.html
http://www.dcregistry.com

It used to be a swamp, but it has grown into a beautiful, vibrant city, full of history and culture.

284
Water

http://ga.water.usgs.gov/edu
http://www.uwex.edu/erc
http://h2o.usgs.gov

Wade right in and learn all about water, conservation, pollution and what you can do to help.

285
Weather

http://www.whnt19.com/kidwx
http://www.usatoday.com/weather/windex.htm
http://www.learner.org/exhibits/weather
http://www.weather.com
Learn all about the weather.

286
Web Site

http://www.lightspan.com
http://library.thinkquest.org
http://www.homepage.com
Teachers and students can create their own Web sites. Lightspan allows a teacher
to integrate the Internet into class work and keep families informed about their
students. ThinkQuest challenges students to create innovative sites.

287
Web Site Evaluation

http://www.ithaca.edu/library/Training/hott.html
http://school.discovery.com/schrockguide/eval.html
http://milton.mse.jhu.edu:8001/research/education/net.html
Since anyone can have a Web site, how can you be assured the content is valid?
These sites will help you become a good editor and reviewer while surfing the Web.

288
Whales

http://www.whaleclub.com
This Web site is designed for whale enthusiasts. You'll find facts, news and pictures.

289
Wild Life

http://www.panda.org/kids/kids.htm
This organization directs its conservation efforts toward three goals: protecting endangered spaces, saving endangered species and addressing global threats.

290
Women

http://www.nmwh.org
http://www.womenswire.com
http://www.ivillage.com
http://www.women.com
http://www.digital-women.com
http://www.wwwomen.com

These sites are dedicated to all aspect of women's lives—home, work, play, health, politics and more.

291
Words

http://www.marleys.com
http://www.puzzlepage.com
http://www.oed.com/wordofday.htm
http://www.wisdom.com

When you use words properly and effectively, the result can be a thing of beauty. Enjoy these sites that challenge your knowledge of words.

292
Words, New

http://www.oed.com/readers
Many of us take words for granted, but it is serious business for the Oxford English Dictionary. You can even play a part in adding new words to this famous dictionary.

293
Worksheets

http://www.freeworksheets.com
Obtain worksheets for all disciplines of education.

294
World Wide Web

http://www.isoc.org/internet/history
http://ww.hcc.hawaii.edu/guide/www.guide.html
Get a history lesson about the Internet.

295
Writing

http://www.inkspot.com
http://www.researchpaper.com/writing.html
http://www.kidpub.org/kidpub
http://www.kidnews.com
These sites have tips for the amateur and professional writer.

296
X-Ray

http://chandra.harvard.edu/edu/index.html
http://www.colorado.edu/physics/2000//xray
Whether you're investigating a broken bone or a solar system zillions of miles away,
X-rays can be very useful.

297
Year

http://www.calendarhome.com
http://www.hemelweb.freeserve.co.uk/birthday.htm
http://www.noblenet.org/year.htm
These sites have interesting facts about time and dates.

298
Youth

http://www.infosprts.com
http://www.usdoj.gov/kidspage
http://www.iyhf.org/iyhf/tpage.html
http://home.concepts.nl/~oprins/yh.html
Get valuable information for and about our youth from the Department of Justice, youth sports leagues and hostels.

299
Zodiac

http://www.easyscopes.com
http://www.zodiachouse.com
http://www.astrology.net
Astrology is a huge hobby and business. Enjoy your time with the stars.

300
Zoo

http://www.si.edu/natzoo
http://www.avma.org/netvet/e-zoo.htm
http://www.zooweb.net/education.htm
Find a zoo to visit or an animal to learn about with these great zoo resources.

INDEX (BY SITE NUMBER)

INDEX (BY SITE NUMBER)

INDEX (BY SITE NUMBER)

The Incredible Newsletter

If you are enjoying this book, you can also arrange to receive a steady stream of more "incredible Internet things," delivered directly to your e-mail address.

The Leebow Letter, Ken Leebow's weekly e-mail newsletter, provides new sites, updates on existing ones and information about other happenings on the Internet.

For more details about *The Leebow Letter* and how to subscribe, visit us at:

WWW.300INCREDIBLE.COM